Our Human
Footprint

PIONEER EDITION

By Barbara H. Seeber

CONTENTS

Our Human

n Footprint

How much does one person
change the planet? The author
wanted to find out. All those
T-shirts, burgers, and long
showers really add up.

By Barbara H. Seeber

I'm not a litterbug. *I don't trash the planet. I think going green is great. But here's the truth. I had no idea how the things I do add up.*

This is called my human footprint. That's the stuff I buy, use, or throw away. Everything I do affects Earth. That's both good news and bad news.

Trash Travels

Here is the bad news. Each person in the United States throws out a lot of trash. One person throws out more than two kilograms of trash every day. That is almost five pounds!

Most trash is put underground in **landfills**. It sits there until it decays. That can take hundreds of years or even thousands of years.

Some trash is burned in big ovens. This sends smoke and chemicals into the air.

Trash can wash down storm drains. It ends up in rivers and oceans. Hikers drop trash when they climb mountains. Mount Everest is the highest mountain in the world. It is also the highest trash dump!

We also use a lot of natural resources. We use oil for gasoline and plastic. We mine coal for **energy**. We use aluminum for cans. We use water to grow crops and to take showers.

The average person in the U.S. uses a lot in a lifetime. See some of it below.

5,054 newspapers

Americans are 5 percent of the world's population. But we use 26 percent of the world's energy.

Hot Air

A person also has a **carbon footprint**. That's how much carbon dioxide (CO_2) each person puts into the air. We put out a lot of CO_2 when we burn coal, oil, or gas. We use these fuels every day to drive our cars and turn on lights. Each American family puts about 68 kilograms of CO_2 into the air every day. That's 150 pounds.

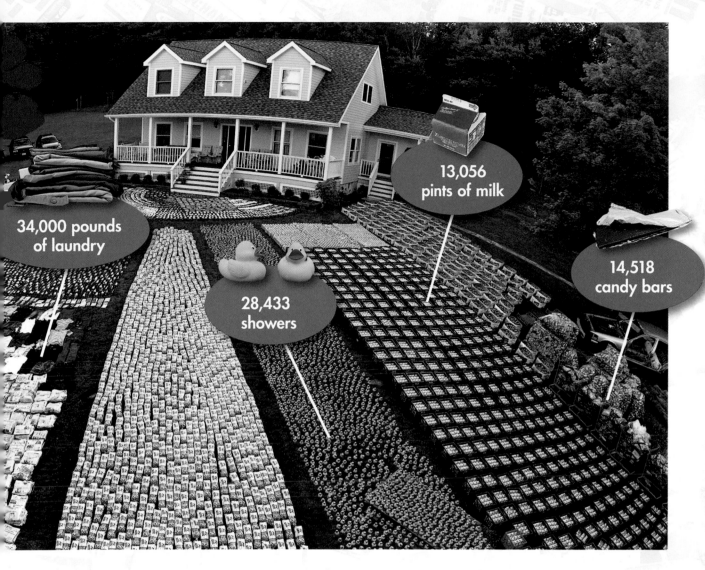

34,000 pounds of laundry

13,056 pints of milk

28,433 showers

14,518 candy bars

Keeping Track

This may sound bad. But there is good news. I can do something about it! I don't have to throw away so much. I can use fewer resources. I can use less energy, too. I don't have to be a Bigfoot. I can shrink my footprint.

First, I have to know how big my footprint is. What do I do every day? How much trash do I make? How much energy and natural resources do I use? I'll keep track. I think I'm in for some surprises!

Trash Pile. *People in the U.S. make a lot of trash. Sometimes, they have to send it to other countries.*

Down the Drain. *One person uses about 380 liters (100 gallons) of water each day in the U.S.*

Fast Food Trash. *Americans eat a lot of fast food. The wrappers and boxes end up in landfills.*

In the Morning

First, I check my email. Oh no! I left the computer on all night. That wastes energy.

The computer uses energy even when it's turned off. That's called vampire power. You can stop it, though. Unplug the computer. I unplug my other electronic stuff, too.

Next stop is my shower. I love long, hot showers. But today my shower is lukewarm and short. It wasn't so bad. And I saved water and energy.

Then I decided to bike to work. The average U.S. car puts about a pound of CO_2 in the air per mile. Using my own energy is good for me. It's good for the planet, too.

Lunch Lessons

It's time for lunch. It's in a bag I can reuse. That's a change. I put my sandwich in a plastic bag last week. I threw it away after I ate. I tossed my plastic water bottle, too. I didn't **litter**. But I created trash. That's not great.

It takes 12 million gallons of oil to make plastic bags for a year. That's a lot of natural resources.

Americans throw away 100 billion plastic bags a year. Many end up in landfills. Many people **recycle** bottles. But others don't. So most plastic bottles end up in landfills, too. They take one thousand years to decay.

Plastic factories use a lot of energy. They make a lot of CO_2, too.

Need or Want?

I ride my bike to the mall. Look at that cute orange T-shirt! I want it. But you need cotton and chemicals to make the shirt. It also takes hundreds of gallons of water. And this one came from China. That's thousands of miles away! Sigh. I'll buy it when I really need new clothes.

I also decide not to buy a new cell phone. Chemicals in old cell batteries can be a problem. They can go into soil and water. That causes pollution. It's a good thing cell phones can be recycled. That's what I'll do when I really need a new one.

Now I'm hungry. I grab a quick burger. Yum! But I look down. I see a paper bag. I see a cup. I see a straw, a wrapper, and a napkin. The trash adds up.

Do You Need It? *It takes chemicals to make one T-shirt. It also takes hundreds of gallons of water.*

How is the burger made? The cows need food and water. Then people need to make the bread. They also have to ship, store, and cook the food. That takes a lot of resources!

Seeing the Light

I go home. I replace my 60-watt light bulbs with 15-watt ones. These use less energy. They last longer, too.

It's time to review my day. I made a few mistakes. But I also made good choices. I threw away less trash. I used less energy. I used fewer of Earth's resources. These small things make a difference. I feel happy. My footprint is smaller today.

Extreme Recycling

I knew it would not be easy to shrink my footprint. At times, I wonder if the little things I do make a difference. Then I remember. I'm not alone.

Many people are helping around the world. We can make a difference when we work together.

Some New Jersey college students started a recycling company in 2001. They looked at the nation's trash. They saw a way to make money.

They collect trash from about 20,000 schools. What do they do with all the drink pouches, snack bags, and cookie wrappers? They make toys and school supplies!

Cereal boxes become notebooks. Newspapers turn into pencils. Cookie wrappers are now kites. I'm glad someone's turning trash into treasure.

Trash People

One German artists turns trash into art. He makes life-sized figures. He uses cans for faces. Computers are the bodies. Cups, bottles, and cell phones make the legs and arms.

This artist puts his Trash People all over the world. What do you think he's saying with his art?

Picked Clean

There is a factory in Sydney, Australia. It takes apart trash. Trucks bring in the garbage. Machines empty bags of trash. Workers get rid of dangerous chemicals. Metals go into one bin. Paper and plastic go into other bins.

The rest goes into a tank. Some trash becomes a gas. Some becomes plant food. By the end, 75 percent of the trash is recycled. Only 25 percent of the trash is left over. It gets buried in a landfill.

Trash People. *An artist makes art from trash. These Trash People stand in the Swiss Alps.*

New Again. *People reuse candy wrappers. They make bags. They also recycle glass to make bracelets.*

1. Bike, walk, or carpool. A car puts about a pound of CO_2 into the air every mile.

2. Turn off the TV when you leave the room. Turn off the lights, too. The energy for an hour of TV puts half a pound of CO_2 in the air.

3. Take short showers. A shower uses five gallons of water every minute.

4. Reuse bags. Plastic bags can end up in the ocean. They make animals sick.

5. Buy things with less packaging. Wrappers make up about one third of everything we throw away.

6. Recycle. Every ton of recycled paper saves 8,000 gallons of water and 17 trees.

7. Plant a tree. One tree takes in about 48 pounds of CO_2 a year.

WORDWISE

carbon footprint: amount of carbon dioxide a person puts into the air

energy: power from fuel that makes machines work

landfill: trash that is buried and covered with dirt

litter: leave paper or trash on the ground

recycle: put things through a process so they can be used again

HOW BIG Is Your FOOTPRINT?

What you use, buy, and throw away changes Earth. This is called your human footprint. How your footprint changes Earth is up to you.

Save Water

We use water to make almost everything. How much water does it take to make a dollar of something? Scientists found out. To make one dollar of cotton, it takes 4,291 liters of water. That is 1,300 gallons! What about one dollar of electricity? It takes 1,703 liters, or 450 gallons, of water.

Save Energy

You can make a difference. Do you use plastic bags? Most people do.

Try reusable bags instead of plastic ones. They save energy and cut down on trash.

People carry groceries in plastic bags. They put their lunch in a plastic bag. They put trash in plastic bags. All that plastic adds up. The resources used to make the bags add up, too.

People use between 500 billion and a trillion plastic bags each year. That many plastic grocery bags would stretch from Earth to the moon and back again 400 times!

It takes a lot of energy to make all those bags. In fact, it takes 12 million gallons of oil to make a year's worth of plastic bags for the United States.

Don't use a plastic bag you will throw away. Use a reusable bag. That will save energy. It will also cut down on the amount of trash you throw out.

Reduce Waste

You can also buy things with less plastic and paper packaging. Make sure to recycle the packaging, too. This saves trees and water. One ton of recycled paper saves 17 trees and 30,283 liters (8,000 gallons) of water.

It is a big job to care for Earth. Yet it can start with you. You decide what to buy. You decide what to recycle. And you decide what to reuse. You can change your human footprint. We can all make the right decisions. Then we will make a big difference!

EARTH

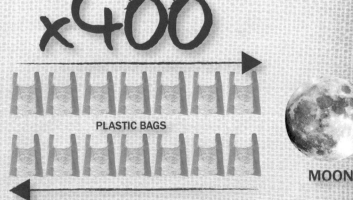

x400

PLASTIC BAGS

MOON

Long Distance. *One trillion plastic bags would stretch from Earth to the moon and back 400 times.*

Reduce, Reuse, Recycle

Find out how to shrink your human footprint. Then answer the questions.

1 What three things make up a person's human footprint?

2 What happens to trash after people throw it away?

3 What are the three best ways to shrink your human footprint? Tell why you think so.

4 What things do people make from recycled trash?

5 How does the diagram on page 11 help you understand the number of plastic bags that people use every year?